W9-BHA-589

The GROSS AND GOOFY Body

Now Hear This!

The Secrets of Ears and Hearing

By Melissa Stewart

Illustrated by Janet Hamlin

mc Marshall Cavendish
Benchmark
New York

This book was made possible,

in part, by a grant from the

Society of Children's Book Writers and Illustrators.

Marshall Cavendish Benchmark
99 White Plains Road
Tarrytown, NY 10591-5502
www.marshallcavendish.us

All websites were available and accurate when this book was sent to press.

Library of Congress Cataloging-in-Publication Data
Stewart, Melissa.
Now hear this! : the secrets of ears and hearing / by Melissa Stewart.
p. cm. — (The gross and goofy body)
Includes index.
Summary: "Provides comprehensive information on the role ears and hearing play in the body science of humans and animals"— Provided by publisher.
ISBN 978-0-7614-4161-8
1. Ears—Juvenile literature. 2. Hearing--Juvenile literature I. Title.
QP462.2.S74 2010
612.8'5—dc22
2008033565

Photo research by Tracey Engel

Cover photo: © bilderlounge/Lisa Penn/Alamy

The photographs in this book are used by permission and through the courtesy of:
Alamy: Ilene MacDonald, 15 (top); Qrt, 27; Redmond Durrell, 33; Dave Marsden, 40; Jason Roberts, 41 (right, bottom). *Getty Images:* National Geographic/Beverly Joubert, 5; Photonica/Lisa Spindler Photography Inc., 7 (right); Stone/Christopher Robbins, 9 (top); National Geographic/Roy Toft, 9 (bottom); Photonica/VEER Scott Barrow, 10; Taxi/Kin Images, 12; National Geographic/Karine Aigner, 16; Stone/Paul Avis, 18; Thomas Starke, 19; National Geographic/Klaus Nigge, 20; Photographer's Choice/Gail Shumway, 21 (top); AFP, 21 (bottom); De Agostini Picture Library/DEA PICTURE LIBRARY, 39. *iStockphoto:* Liza McCorkle, 4; Christopher Badzioch, 32 (bottom); Michael Pettigrew, 32 (top); KonovalikovAndrey, 41 (top, left). *Photo Researchers, Inc.:* Phanie, 7 (left); SPL, 37. *Shutterstock:* Francois Etienne du Plessis, 15 (bottom); Stephen Pamment, 23; Ivan Histand, 25; Wendy Kaveney Photography, 29 (top); Ryan M. Bolton, 29 (bottom); dellison, 30; HTuller, 35; Cindy Davenport, 41 (right, top).

Editor: Joy Bean
Publisher: Michelle Bisson
Art Director: Anahid Hamparian
Series Designer: Daniel Roode

Printed in Malaysia

1 3 5 6 4 2

CONTENTS

THREE CHEERS FOR EARS

Ears. They're those funny-looking things sticking out of the sides of your head. They're full of ridges and valleys and dark, hidden alleys. Near the bottom, a small tunnel disappears into your head.

Ears are a good place to rest eyeglasses or hang earrings. And they're perfectly shaped for tucking away loose strands of hair. But that's not all your hear-oic ears can do for you. You'll be amazed at all the ways ears make life better for you—and for other animals, too.

A fennec fox lives in the desert, but staying cool is no problem. On hot afternoons it releases body heat through the thin skin on its enormous ears.

In the chilly Arctic large ears could freeze and fall off. That's why a polar bear has small ears covered with thick fur. When the bear goes swimming, it lays its ears flat against its head so water can't trickle in.

Want to know how an elephant feels? Just look at its ears. When an elephant feels calm or safe, it holds its ears flat against its body. But when an elephant is angry or frightened, it holds its ears out straight.

LOVE THOSE LOBES

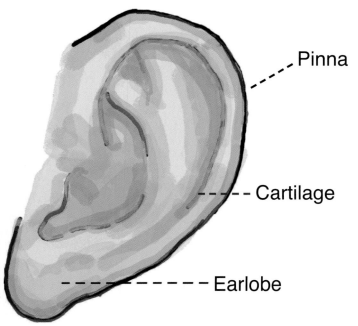

Pinna

Cartilage

Earlobe

When you look at a person's ear, what you see is the **pinna**. The upper edges are soft and squishy. The stiff, solid center is made of **cartilage**—a tough material similar to the gristle in meat. The earlobe at the bottom is a bulging blob of floppy flesh.

Some people's earlobes are connected to their heads. But most earlobes dangle free. Which kind do you have? How about your friends and family members?

Like eye color and hair color, earlobe type is a genetic trait. It's passed on from one generation to the next. If both your parents have earlobes that hang free, yours could be attached. But if they both have attached earlobes, yours must be, too.

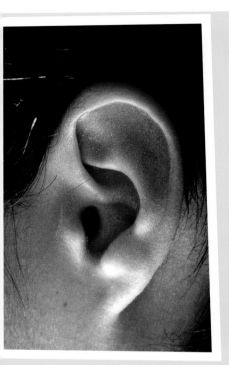

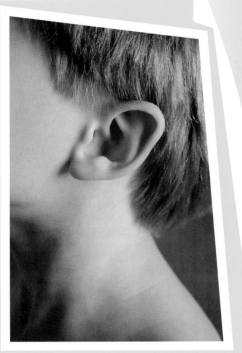

Attached earlobe. 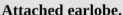   **Detached earlobe.**

Look Out for Lines

Know anyone with wrinkly lines on their earlobes? Some scientists say they're a sign of heart disease. Nobody knows what causes the curious creases. They might form when **blood vessels** in a person's earlobes collapse.

According to the *Guinness Book of World Records,* Monte Pierce can stretch his earlobes to a length of nearly 5 inches (13 centimeters). Using them like a slingshot, he can launch coins up to 10 feet (3 meters).

PINNAS AT WORK

Using your fingertip, gently trace the maze of twists and turns in the upper half of your pinna. Now look at your finger. You'll probably see a wad of greasy, grimy gunk lodged underneath your fingernail. Ew! Gross!

Scrape out the gunk and take a closer look. It's a mangled mash of dirt and dead skin cells mixed with sweat and oils from your skin. If your pinna didn't trap it, all that yucky stuff could end up in your **ear canal**. Then you'd have trouble hearing.

But that's not all your pinnas do for you. Their most important job is collecting sounds and funneling them into your head.

Hairy and Scary

How are your dad's pinnas different from yours? They're bigger, of course. And they're probably hairier, too. As men get older, more and more hair sprouts from their pinnas. According to the *Guinness Book of World Records*, Radhakant Bajpai of India has the longest ear hair ever measured. It's more than 5 inches (13 cm) long.

How does a giraffe wash its pinnas? With the *slobbery* spit that coats its 21-inch (53-cm) long tongue.

LET'S HEAR IT FOR THE EARS

Try this. Go outside and find a pebble. Fill a large bowl with water and toss in the pebble. What do you see? Tiny waves rippling out in every direction.

The same thing happens when the bell rings at the end of recess or a car horn blasts as you ride home from school. It even happens when your best friend belts out the loudest

Burrrp!

burp you've ever heard. Invisible waves of sound erupt from your friend's mouth and spread through the air.

The air all around Earth is full of **sound waves**. But you only hear noises when the waves bump into your pinnas and get funneled into your ear canals.

Oversized Ears

Most parts of your body will stop growing by the time you graduate from high school, but your ears never stop. Between the ages of twenty and seventy, a person's pinnas grow about 0.5 inches (1.3 cm).

What's That Sound?

You know that soft, swishing noise you hear when you hold a spiral seashell up to your ear? Some people say it's the sound of crashing ocean waves. But that's not really true. What you're hearing is sound waves bouncing around inside the shell.

LOUD AND CLEAR

Which is louder: your friend's whisper when she tells you a secret or your sister's scream when you soak her with the garden hose? The scream, of course. But how do your ears know?

Sound waves are shaped just like ocean waves. The height of sound waves determines their loudness.

When tall sound waves from a jackhammer or a siren pound against your pinna and all the parts inside your ear, you hear a loud sound. When shorter sound waves enter your ear, you hear softer sounds, such as a gentle breeze or a cat licking its fur.

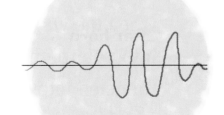

This sound wave diagram shows a loud noise moving toward you.

Scientists measure the loudness of a sound in **decibels** (dB). Humans can hear sounds as soft as 1 dB and as loud as 150 dB. Anything louder causes severe pain.

Sound	Loudness (dB)
Whisper	20
Ticking watch	20
Gentle breeze	30
Talking	60
Highway traffic	70
Alarm clock	80
Lawn mower	95
Crying child	110
Car horn	110
Chain saw	110
Ambulance siren	120
Jet airplane	130
Rock concert	140

Did You Know?

If you listen to sounds above 100 dB for too long, you could damage your ears. That's why many rock musicians have lost some of their hearing.

A PERFECT PAIR

Cover one ear with your hand, shut your eyes, and listen. What do you hear? Try to guess where the sounds are coming from. Not so easy, is it?

Now try listening with both ears. When your ears work together, your brain has no trouble pinpointing the source of a sound.

The instant you hear an ambulance siren, your ears and brain go to work. They analyze the sound waves to figure out where the ambulance is.

If your left ear collects taller (louder) sound waves than your right ear, your brain knows the ambulance is to your left. And if the waves are getting taller and taller, your brain knows the ambulance is moving toward you. Even if you can't see the ambulance, your brain knows exactly where it is driving up the street on your left.

Biggest Ears

African elephants have the biggest ears on Earth. They're about the size of the blanket on a twin bed.

Sharpest Hearing

Owls probably have the sharpest hearing. They can hear at least five times better than humans. With ears like that, mice and rabbits don't stand a chance!

WATCH 'EM WIGGLE

Some animals' ears are even better at locating sounds than yours are. That's because they can move their ears without turning their heads.

When a cat or dog, horse or rabbit hears a noise, its ears stick up straight. The ears pivot to the right and left until they pinpoint the source. What a great trick!

You can't move your ears like a rabbit or a cat, but you can learn to wiggle them. What's the secret? Knowing how to control the muscles above and behind your ears.

This wild cat is listening carefully for signs of danger.

You may already move your ears a tiny bit when you smile, raise an eyebrow, or open your mouth in surprise. Look in a mirror to find out. Once you locate the right muscles, keep on practicing. Soon you'll be the best ear wiggler in your class.

Pivoting Pinnas

Want to hear as well as a cat? Cup your hands around the outsides of your ears and practice swiveling them in and out, up and down. This will help you pinpoint sounds. It'll also make your pinnas bigger, so they can collect more sound waves.

HIGHS AND LOWS

What does the rumble of distant thunder have in common with your dad's snoring and the soothing sound of a bass guitar? They're all low and deep. These noises have a low **pitch** because the sound waves they give off hit your ears slowly. The sound waves from high-pitched noises, such as the screech of car brakes or your soccer coach's whistle, are closer together.

Scientists measure pitch in hertz (Hz). You can probably hear sounds with pitches between 20 and 20,000 Hz. But as you get older, you'll lose some of that range. By the time you're fifty years old, you may only be able to hear sounds with pitches between 50 and 8,000 Hz.

Pitch Switching

Men usually have deeper voices than women and children. The average adult male voice has a pitch of 125 Hz. The average pitch for the voices of women and children is about 225 Hz.

If you're a boy, your voice will deepen when you're around fourteen years old. That's when you'll go through puberty—all the body changes that make you an adult.

HOW LOW CAN THEY GO?

Some animals can hear sounds that you can't. That's because their ears are tuned in to sounds waves with very high or very low pitches.

Many large animals can make and hear low, rumbling sounds that travel long distances through air, water, and even the ground. Elephants, alligators, whales, giraffes, hippopotamuses, and rhinoceroses all use these **infrasounds** to communicate short, simple messages, such as "I'm over here!" or "Danger!"

Scientists have spent the most time studying elephant infrasounds. They know that the giant beasts' low-pitched calls can travel up to 6 miles (9.7 kilometers) through the air and more than 20 miles (32 km) through the ground. Now, that's incredible!

Animal	Range of Pitches It Can Hear (Hz)
Elephant	1 to 20,000
Goldfish	5 to 2,000
Horse	30 to 40,000
Dog	40 to 46,000
Cat	100 to 32,000
Grasshopper	100 to 50,000
Sea lion	200 to 55,000
Dolphin	200 to 150,000
Rat	1,000 to 50,000
Mouse	1,000 to 100,000
Bat	1,000 to 150,000
Moth	1,000 to 240,000

Infrasounds Inside

You can't hear infrasounds, but that doesn't mean your body doesn't make them. The sounds of your blood flowing and your muscles moving are below your range of hearing.

ECHO, ECHO, ECHO

What do bats and dolphins have in common? They both make and hear **ultrasounds**—noises so high-pitched that people can't hear them. And they use sounds—not sight—to understand their world.

As dolphins swim, they make a steady clicking noise. And flying bats constantly call out into the night. When these sounds hit something, they bounce back. Each returning echo gives the animals a more complete picture of their surroundings. If a dolphin detects a rock, it glides around it. And if a bat darts past a tasty insect, it quickly changes direction and chases after the **prey**.

For **echolocation** to work, bats and dolphins need ears that are perfectly in tune with their clicks and calls. Dolphins don't have **outer ears**. The echoes they hear travel through their jaws to their **inner ears**. Bats' pinnas are full of wrinkles and folds, so they can detect even the smallest sounds.

Did You Know?

People can hear the echolocation calls that a few bats make, but most of them are out of our hearing range. Good thing, too. Imagine holding a blasting smoke detector just 4 inches (10 cm) from your ear. That's how loud some bat calls are.

INTO THE TUNNEL

When you look at the opening to your ear canal, it's hard to imagine what's inside. That dark little tunnel is about half as long as your pinky finger. At the far end sound waves crash into your **eardrum**—a thin, skinlike membrane that separates your **outer ear** from your **middle ear**.

Soft, sensitive skin lines the surface of your ear canal. Just below the surface, dozens of small sacs called **cerumen glands** are constantly cranking out a fresh supply of icky earwax. The wax oozes through tiny tubes and seeps into your ear canal through pitlike pores.

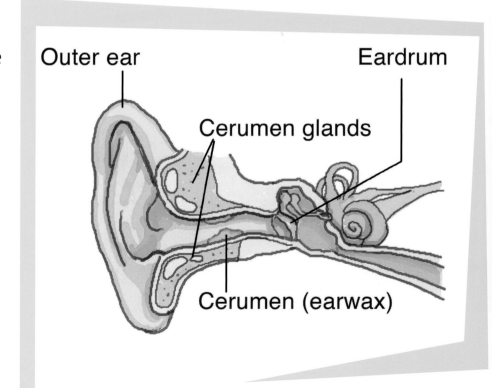

Outer ear

Eardrum

Cerumen glands

Cerumen (earwax)

If your ancestors came from Europe or Africa, your earwax probably forms soft, sticky, yellow clumps. But if your ancestors were Asian or Native American, your earwax probably forms hard, crusty, gray flakes.

Did You Know?

Humans aren't the only animals with earwax. Many animals have it. In whales earwax builds up in layers year after year. When scientists find a dead whale, they can tell how long it lived by counting the layers of wax inside its ears.

A white beluga whale.

THE WONDERS OF WAX

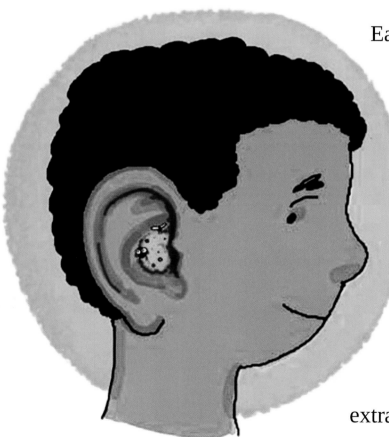

Earwax coats the walls of your ear canals. It keeps the skin inside your ears moist. And it protects your delicate eardrums by trapping anything that flies, crawls, or gets blown into your ears.

That includes dust, dirt, tiny insects, and even drops of water.

Chemicals in earwax keep you healthy by killing **bacteria**, fungi, and other invaders.

What should you do to get rid of extra earwax? Nothing!

Doctors tell their patients not to use cotton swabs to clean their ears. The swabs can damage your ears.

As new earwax oozes into your ear canal, it pushes old earwax out of the way. Like lumpy oatmeal on a conveyor belt, aged earwax and its load of garbage slowly slides out to your pinna. If it's dry and flaky, it falls out of your ear. If it's wet and sticky, you rinse it away as you wash your hair.

Earwax Solves Crimes

You've probably heard of **DNA**. It's the genetic material inside your cells that codes for all your body's traits. Like fingerprints, everyone's DNA is different, so police can use it to solve crimes. Police often find traces of DNA at crime scenes. It's in blood and hair, spit and snot. In one case they identified a suspect using DNA from a ball of earwax stuck to the earpiece of a two-way radio.

ITTY-BITTY BONES

Hold out your hand and look at your pinky. Your eardrum is about the size of the fingernail on the end. But it's even thinner.

When sound waves hit the tightly stretched membrane, it vibrates, or moves back and forth. As your eardrum shimmies and shakes, three itty-bitty bones inside your middle ear start to move, too.

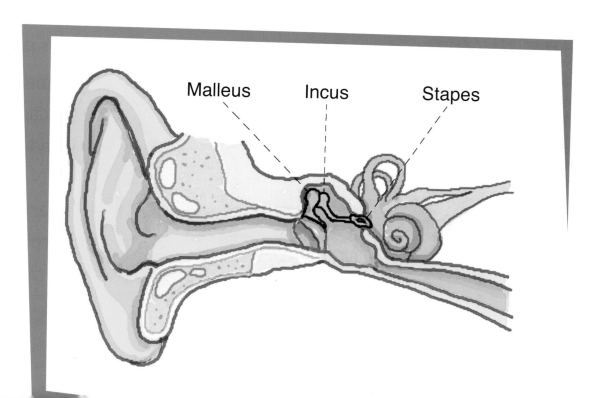

Malleus   Incus   Stapes

First the vibrations pass through your **malleus**, then your **incus**, and finally your **stapes**. All three bones are smaller than a baked bean, but the stapes is the smallest of all. It's the smallest bone in your whole body.

Ever notice the strange circles around a frog's eyes? They're eardrums. Frogs don't have pinnas, but their enormous eardrums work just like yours.

What's in a Name?

The bones in your middle ear are named for their shapes. *Malleus* is the Latin word for "hammer." *Incus* is a Latin word that means "anvil," a heavy iron block used to shape metals after they've been heated. *Stapes* means "stirrup" in Latin. A stirrup is a loop that hangs from a horse's saddle and supports the rider's foot.

POPPING POWER

Try this. Close your mouth and swish your tongue back and forth. Let a large puddle of spit build up inside your mouth. Now listen closely as you swallow.

Did you hear a tiny click? That's your **Eustachian tube** doing its job. Every time you swallow, yawn, or chew, the tiny tube opens up so air can move back and forth between your middle ear and your throat. It's your body's way of making sure the air pressure inside and outside your ear always stays the same.

When you drive up a mountain or take off in an airplane, the air pressure around you changes quickly. Your ears feel clogged. They might even hurt. But then your eustachian tubes come to the rescue. You hear a loud pop as they open wide. Low-pressure air races into your ears while higher-pressure air zooms toward your throat. What a relief!

Stuffy Nose, Stuffy Ears

When you have a cold, the body tissues around your nose can really swell up. Sometimes they block the openings of your eustachian tubes. That can make your ears feel as stuffed up as your nose.

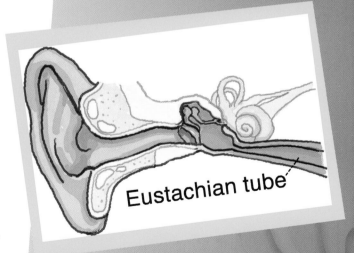

Eustachian tube

INSECT EARS

Insects have ears in all kinds of places.

Green lacewings and some kinds of butterflies have ears on their wings. They're just what these insects need to avoid enemies.

Cicadas, grasshoppers, tiger beetles, and many kinds of moths have ears on the back section of their bodies. Cicadas and grasshoppers use their ears to find mates. Tiger beetles and moths rely on their ears to help them escape from enemies.

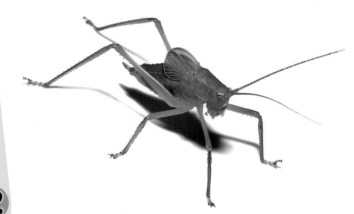

Crickets and katydids have ears on their knees. They're perfect for hearing the mating songs the males make with their wings.

A female tachinid fly's ears are located near the tops of her legs. When she hears a cricket's high-pitched mating call, she flies over her victim and sprays it with **larvae**. The young flies burrow into the cricket and devour it from the inside out. Yuck!

As mosquitoes fly through the air, the ears at the base of their antennae are always alert. You probably hate the whiny sound a mosquito makes with its wings, but it's music to the ears of other mosquitoes. It tells them a friend is close by.

A praying mantis has a single ear on the bottom of its **thorax**. It's tuned in to the high-pitched cries of the insect's worst enemy—the bat.

What's really going on deep inside your ears? To find out, you'd have to slice open your skull and take a look.

Just behind and below each eyeball, you'd see a small, coiled tube that looks like a snail's spiral shell. It's your **cochlea**.

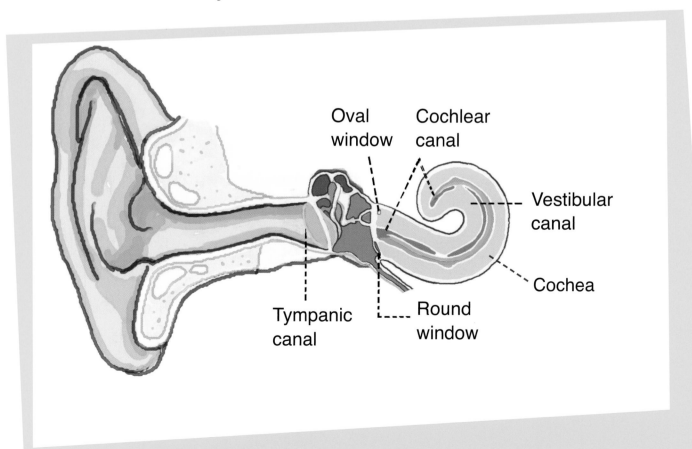

Oval window

Cochlear canal

Vestibular canal

Cochea

Tympanic canal

Round window

As sound vibrations move through your middle ear, the stapes pushes against and then pulls away from your **oval window**.

Each time the oval window bulges forward, fluid inside your **vestibular canal** forms waves.

When the waves reach the center of the spiral, they pass into your **tympanic canal**.

The waves travel outward until they reach the **round window**. As the waves crash against the thin membrane, the membrane quivers and quakes. And sound energy slowly passes out of your ears.

Sandwiched between your vestibular and tympanic canals is a thin tube called the cochlear canal. It's where hearing occurs.

Hearing Twice Sounds Nice

Try this. Talk into a recording device and then play it back. Surprised by what you hear? Normally, you hear sound waves from your mouth in two different ways. Some enter your pinna and pass through your middle ear. Others ricochet off the bones inside your head until they reach your **inner ear**. When the two sounds combine, your voice seems richer and deeper than it does when you listen to it on a recording.

HEAR YE, HEAR YE!

Now take an even closer look at the tiny structures inside your cochlea. They work together to help you hear your dad's goofy jokes and the bell at recess. You also depend on them to hear fire alarms and car horns and your mom's angry voice when she catches you sneaking a cookie before dinner.

As waves of fluid roll through the tympanic canal, they shake the **basilar membrane** lining the bottom of your cochlear canal.

Those vibrations move into the **organ of Corti**, which rests on top of your basilar membrane.

Organ of Corti

Hearing cells

Cochlear nerve

Basilar membrane

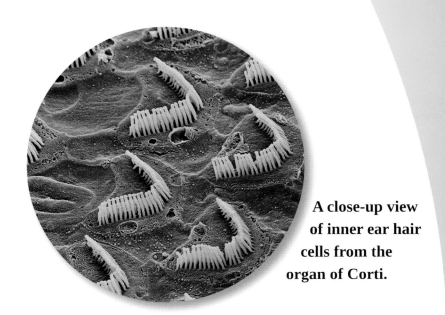

A close-up view of inner ear hair cells from the organ of Corti.

The organ of Corti contains more than 20,000 hearing cells. Supersensitive hairs at the top of each hearing cell detect the vibrations and turn them into electrical signals.

Those signals travel through the **cochlear nerve** to your brain. Your brain interprets the signals and sends out messages that tell your body how to react.

Protein Power

How do the hairs on hearing cells change sound vibrations into electrical signals? A **protein** called prestin does the job. Scientists are trying to coat space suits with the power-producing protein. They hope that as astronauts move, the prestin will pump out enough juice to charge batteries and run small devices. One day these special space suits might be used on Mars!

A BALANCING ACT

Your inner ear does more than hear. It also helps you keep your balance. To understand how, you'll need to take another look at some of the tiny structures deep inside your head.

Your oval window opens into a large central area called the vestibule. The **vestibule** contains two small sacs filled with a syrupy liquid and tiny, solid crystals. When you hold your head upright, the crystals spread out evenly. If you tip your head, the crystals slide to the lowest part of each sac. Tiny hairs lining the insides of the sacs send nerve signals to your brain. That's how you always know the position of your head.

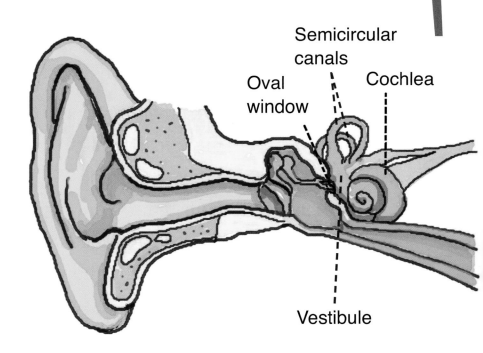

Semicircular canals

Cochlea

Oval window

Vestibule

Your cochlea branches off to one side of the vestibule, and three long, looping semicircular canals branch off on the other side. When you turn around, lie down, or stand on your head, fluid inside your **semicircular canals** flows in the direction of the movement. Then tiny hairs inside the canals send your brain information about the position and movement of your entire body. That's how you keep your balance.

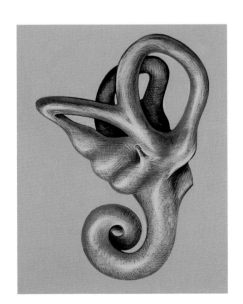

Fluid inside your three semicircular canals (top) helps you keep your balance.

Mixed Messages

When you spin in circles, the fluid in your semicircular canals spins, too. When you stop, the fluid keeps on moving. Your eyes tell your brain that you're standing still. But your ears say you're still spinning. Those mixed messages confuse your brain, and you end up feeling dizzy.

WHERE ARE THEIR EARS?

From enjoying a good joke to protecting us from danger, it's hard to believe all the ways our ears help us every day. And we aren't alone. Many other animals depend on ears, too — even though we can't always see them.

When sound waves strike a snake's scaly skin, vibrations move through the muscles and bones inside its head. Eventually, the sound messages are funneled into the reptile's inner ears.

Some owls have tufts of feathers on top of their heads. The feathers look like pinnas, but they actually have nothing to do with hearing. Sound waves enter a bird's head through two small holes hidden under a thick layer of feathers.

You can't see a fish's ears either. That's because it doesn't have any—at least not on the outside of its body. A fish doesn't need pinnas because sound waves have no trouble passing through its body to its inner ears.

Ear ID

How can you tell the difference between sea lions and true seals? By looking at their ears. Sea lions have small flaps of skin covering their ear canals, but you can see straight into a true seal's ears.

A sea lion.

A seal.

bacteria—Tiny, one-celled living things that reproduce by dividing.

basilar membrane—A thin, skin-like layer that separates the cochlea's tympanic canal and cochlear canal.

cartilage—The flexible material that gives your pinnas their shape.

cerumen gland—A tiny sac that produces and releases cerumen, or earwax.

cochlea—A coiled, snail-shaped structure in the inner ear. It converts sound vibrations from the middle ear into electrical signals, which travel to the brain.

cochlear nerve—A large nerve that carries sound messages from the cochlea to the brain.

DNA (deoxyribonucleic acid)—A molecule with instructions that direct all the activities in a cell. It is passed from parent to child during reproduction.

ear canal—The tube that leads from the pinna to the eardrum.

eardrum— The membrane that separates the outer ear from the middle ear. It vibrates when sound waves hit.

echolocation— A sensory system that involves sending out sounds and listening to their echoes. Animals that echolocate can detect the size, distance, and texture of objects by interpreting the echoes that bounce off those objects.

Eustachian tube—The tube that connects the middle ear to the back of the throat. It allows air to flow into and out of the middle ear.

fungi—Living things made of many cells that are neither a plant nor an animal. Some fungi can make you sick.

incus—One of the three tiny bones in the middle ear. It transfers sound vibrations from the malleus to the stapes.

infrasound—A sound with a pitch so low, human ears can't detect it.

inner ear—The area of the ear beyond the oval window.

larva (pl. larvae)—The second stage in the life of amphibians and many invertebrates, including flies and some other insects.

malleus—One of the tiny bones in the middle ear. It fits into the eardrum and transfers sound vibrations to the incus.

organ of Corti—A structure inside the cochlear canal that contains hearing cells.

outer ear—The area of the ear that includes the pinna and ear canal.

oval window—The membrane that separates the middle ear from the inner ear.

pinna—The part of the ear visible on the outside of some animals' heads.

pitch—A quality of sound determined by the frequency with which sound waves strike the ear.

protein—A molecule that speeds up chemical reactions, repairs damaged cells, ands builds new bones, teeth, hair, muscles, and skin.

round window—A membrane that releases sound energy from the ear.

semicircular canal—One of the three loop-shaped structures in the inner ear. The semicircular canals detect changes in the position of the body, so the brain can direct muscles to maintain balance.

sound wave—The form sound energy takes as it moves through solids, liquids, and gases.

stapes—The smallest bone in the human body. It transfers sound vibrations from the incus to the oval window.

thorax—The middle section of an insect's body, where the legs and wings are attached.

tympanic canal—One of the tubes in the cochlea. It carries waves it receives from the vestibular canal to the round window.

ultrasound—A sound with a pitch so high, human ears can't detect it.

vestibular canal—One of the canals in the cochlea. As the oval window pushes into the fluid-filled vestibular canal, waves form.

vestibule—A structure in the inner ear. It contains two small sacs that sense changes in the position of the head.

A NOTE ON SOURCES

Dear Readers,

I've written about ears and hearing before, so I knew quite a bit about the topic before I began to work on this book. But I also knew that *Now Hear This!* would look at ears in a whole new way.

I wanted kids to know that not all earwax is the same and that anyone can learn to wiggle his or her ears. I also worked hard to include the latest information about how scientists are using ear proteins to design better space suits and how police are using earwax to solve crimes.

I started my research by reading books. To understand how ears work, I looked at two newly published college textbooks and relied heavily on articles in scientific journals. I also read popular magazine articles and looked for information on the Internet. Along the way I learned that scientists can use earwax to determine a whale's age and that human ears never stop growing.

My final step was to speak to doctors and scientists doing ear research. These interviews ensure that the book includes the most up-to-date information about insect hearing and how elephants use their ears.

— Melissa Stewart

FIND OUT MORE

BOOKS

Amazing Animals of the World. New York: Scholastic Library, 2006.

Gibson, Gary. *Hearing and Sounds.* Brookfield, CT: Copper Beech Press, 2008.

Landau, Elaine. *The Sense of Hearing.* New York: Children's Press, 2008.

Stewart, Melissa. *How Do Bats Fly in the Dark?* Benchmark Book, 2008.

WEBSITES

Did You Know There's a Jawbone in Your Ear?
Scientists from the Smithsonian Institution's Natural History Museum explain how ears evolved over time.
http://www.mnh.si.edu/mammals/pages/what/earbones.htm

Guinness World Records
Up-to-date information on some of the strangest world's records you can imagine.
http://www.guinnessworldrecords.com/default.aspx

The Sound Site
Hear some surprising sounds and try some fun activities to learn more about sound.
http://www.smm.org/sound/nocss/top.html

INDEX

Page numbers in **bold** are illustrations.

ABOUT THE AUTHOR

Melissa Stewart has written everything from board books for preschoolers to magazine articles for adults. She is the award-winning author of more than one hundred books for young readers. She serves on the board of advisors of the Society of Children's Book Writers and Illustrators and is a judge for the American Institute of Physics Children's Science Writing Award. Melissa earned a B.S. in biology from Union College and an M.A. in science journalism from New York University. She lives in Acton, Massachusetts, with her husband, Gerard. To learn more about Stewart, please visit her website: www.melissa-stewart.com.

ABOUT THE ILLUSTRATOR

Janet Hamlin has illustrated many children's books, games, newspapers, and even Harry Potter stuff. She is also a court artist. The Gross and Goofy Body is one of her all-time favorite series, and she now considers herself the factoid queen of bodily functions. She lives and draws in New York and loves it.